STRIKE FIVE

An Introduction to Early Classroom Work with Tuned Percussion Instruments

Peter Sidaway

SCHOTT

London · Mainz · New York · Tokyo

ED 12164

©1984
Schott and Co. Ltd,
London
ISBN No. 0 901938 85 8

Reproduced and printed by Halstan & Co. Ltd., Amersham, Bucks., England

STRIKE FIVE

An introduction to early classroom work with tuned percussion instruments.

WHAT THIS BOOK EXPLAINS

....how to choose, play and look after glockenspiels, chime bars, xylophones and metallophones.

....how to progress from rhythmic to melodic work in the classroom

....how to organise simple accompaniments to songs

....how to use tuned percussion instruments with recorders

....how to introduce one note at a time on tuned percussion, and progress gradually to the pentatonic (five-note) scale

It is not assumed that the teacher can play the piano: the book is designed to help the non-specialist teacher particularly.

CONTENTS

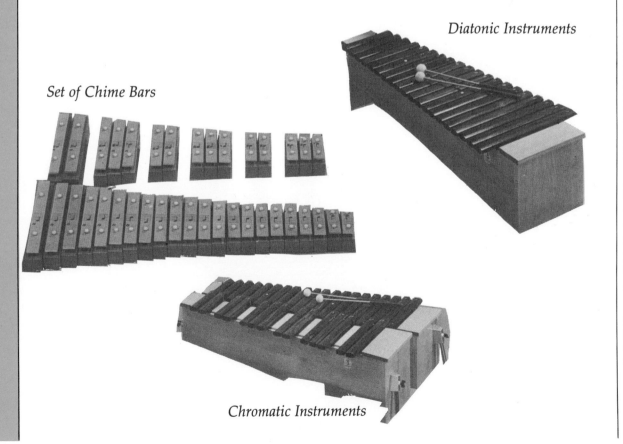

Diatonic Instruments

Set of Chime Bars

Chromatic Instruments

PART ONE: Introducing Tuned Percussion

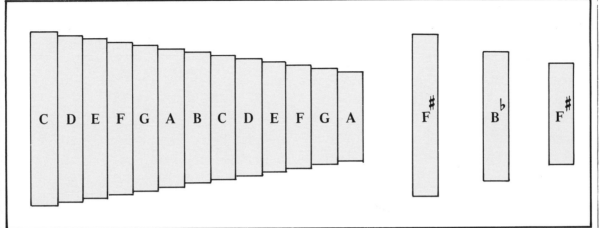

◆ DIATONIC refers to the notes of a particular major (or minor) scale. Most tuned percussion are diatonic to the scale of C.

◆◆ A PERCUSSION instrument is one in which a resonating surface is struck by the player, who uses either his hand (or some other part of the body) or an object, usually a stick or beater.

◆◆◆ CHROMATIC ("colourful") refers to the notes which are not included in the scale in question. F sharp and B flat are not in the scale of C.

A diatonic ◆ tuned percussion ◆◆ instrument normally contains thirteen notes from C to A an octave and a sixth above, and three chromatic ◆◆◆ notes, F♯, B♭ and the octave F♯.

THE NATURE AND CHARACTERISTICS OF THE INSTRUMENTS.

1. The following descriptions refer to the 'Studio 49' instruments illustrated on the previous page, but are applicable to instruments made by most manufacturers. Apart from chime bars, there are three basic families.

2. The table below gives the characteristics of these basic families.

GLOCKENSPIEL is German for 'peal of bells'.

'XYLO' is a Greek prefix meaning "wooden".

	GLOCKENSPIEL	METALLOPHONE	XYLOPHONE
Bars are made of:	Nickel-plated steel	Aluminium alloy (softer than glockenspiel bars)	Rosewood
period of resonance:	medium	long	brief
types (and codes used by Studio 49)	Soprano (SG) Alto (AG)	Soprano (SM) Alto (AM) Bass (BM)	Soprano (SX) Alto (AX) Bass (BX)
The bars are secured by pins and supported over a wooden box divided into resonance chambers.			

HOW TO PLAY THE INSTRUMENTS

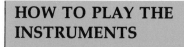

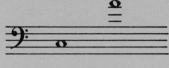

Bass xylophone
Bass metallophone

Alto xylophone
Alto metallophone

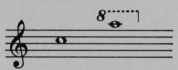

Soprano xylophone
Soprano metallophone
Alto glockenspiel

Soprano glockenspiel

3. Diatonic instruments usually have the following sixteen notes:

4. Music for them is usually written at the pitches indicated above, but only the sounds produced by the bars of the ALTO XYLOPHONE and ALTO METALLOPHONE are at these actual pitches. Thus all the other tuned instruments in the three families are tranposing instruments in that their written and sounding pitches are not identical. The diagram (left) shows this.

5. Although the instruments are called 'Soprano', 'Alto' and 'Bass', there are really four different pitch ranges: the SOPRANO XYLOPHONE and ALTO GLOCKENSPIEL are at the same pitch.

6. Chromatic versions of the instruments are available, containing all diatonic and chromatic notes (i.e. $C^\sharp$, $D^\sharp$, and $G^\sharp$) in addition to the notes supplied on a diatonic instrument. Diatonic xylophones and metallophones can be converted into chromatic instruments by purchasing a separate chromatic box which has the $C^\sharp$, $D^\sharp$ and $G^\sharp$ which the diatonic instruments lack. In the classroom, however, diatonic instruments serve well in most situations.

7. Alto glockenspiels and alto and bass metallophones are available with damping devices which shorten the length of time that the bars vibrate. The damping bar is, in effect, an adjustable support for the ends of the bars nearest the player. When fully in it rests against the body of the instrument.

The further it is withdrawn towards the player, the briefer the sounds of the bars.

HOW TO PLAY
THE INSTRUMENTS

8. Beaters, otherwise called mallets or sticks, are provided with the instruments. In the early stages of playing, use only the proper beaters, one in each hand, and let their heads strike the middle of the bars for the best tone, and rebound at once. Encourage children to 'bounce' them.

9. The usual, but not invariable way to play a melody is to alternate the beaters. In this book, downward stems indicate that the bars corresponding to the notes are to be played with the left hand beater, and upward stems the right hand.

Practise:

10. Set the instruments with the longest bars to the left, horizontally at a suitable height: this is approximately at waist level if you stand, or level with the knees if you are seated. Adjustable legs or instrument tables are available to facilitate this, if required. Sit as close to the instrument as possible, relaxed, holding the elbows away from the body, with gently curving arms. If standing, you should not be quite as close to the instruments,

The three chromatic notes supplied with a diatonic instrument are marked in the diagram.

is sometimes used for the BASS XYLOPHONE to show that it sounds an octave lower than written

The bars of tuned percussion instruments normally rest on a support at their nodal points. Even when a bar is struck there is no vibration at these points. When the damping bar is withdrawn it supports the bars at points at which they do vibrate, and thus shortens the vibration time.

Encourage children to use a beater in each hand, right from the beginning

Posture is important when playing instruments.

HOW TO PLAY THE INSTRUMENTS

neither should you have to bend down. Children sometimes put an instrument on the floor and kneel to play it. If two share a larger instrument, one playing the lower notes and the other the higher, they should be on the same side of the instrument, otherwise the one playing with the short bars to his left will get distorted ideas about pitch conventions (normally playing from left to right equates with going **up**). They should also be close together, side by side, and not one at each end of the instrument.

11. If the children are young or inexperienced, remove all the bars except for those to be used. Both hands should grip a bar to be removed, one at each end, so that it can be lifted straight up, parallel with the instruments.

Avoid bending pins

More about BEATERS

● Each instrument comes with one pair of beaters. Buy two more pairs:
(a) to cover losses
(b) to allow children to hold two in one hand to play a chord
(c) to allow two to play the larger instruments, sitting side by side.

● **Why use two beaters?**
Because
(a) only the simplest music is possible with one beater. To make your point, ask the recalcitrant child to play:

(compare his performance with that of a child using two beaters!)

(b) there is a much stronger feeling of BALANCE, encouraging lightness and flow.
(c) improvisation is easier
(d) distribution of labour between the hands avoids stiffness

● **Beaters are expensive**.
Give someone reponsibility for their distribution and collection.

● **Normally, use the proper beaters for an instrument**.
Use a pair of S4 beaters on a bass xylophone. The lower notes do not respond well to such hard beaters. Try the S4's on a soprano xylophone. They are not hard enough to resonate the higher bars adequately.

● **On the other hand, be experimental when the occasion arises**. Try using objects other than beaters to resonate the bars of an instrument., e.g. beads on a metallophone, or ping-pong balls dropped on to the same instrument, and use 'incorrect' beaters for novel effects.

● **Chords**
To play a two-note chord in the right hand, hold the beaters over the instrument to gauge the distance between their heads in relation to that between the bars to be struck. Insert the index finger at the appropriate spot between the handles, the ends of which should be kept firmly in the hand. [Sliding the finger up and down alters the distance between the beaters.]

Studio 49 Cat No.	Description	Studio 49 Cat No	Description
S1	for glockenspiel and woodblock (wooden head, plastic handle)	S6	for bass metallophones (head wrapped in wool, plastic handle)
S2	for glockenspiel and woodblock (plastic head, plastic handle)	S7	for metallophones (felt head soft, plastic handle)
S3	for bass xylophones (head wrapped in wool, plastic handle)	S8	for metallophones (wooden head with rubber ring, plastic handle)
S4	for xylophones (felt head medium-hard, plastic handle)	S9	for special purposes (wooden head with leather ring, plastic handle)
S5	for xylophones (felt head, hard plastic handle)	S10	for bass metallophones (rubber head soft, plastic handle)

Try this:

R.H. two beaters

HOW TO CARE FOR THE INSTRUMENTS

How to care for instruments

PINS

Always return bent securing pins to the vertical — otherwise the vibration of the bar will be inhibited, and this will result in poor tone quality.

Replacements pins are available from the manufacturer.

RUBBER TUBING

The rubber tubing around the pins and that on which the bars rest will be replaced by the manufacturer when it perishes. Specify the instrument and whether the tubing is for the pins or to support the bars, when requesting it.

BARS

Glockenspiel bars may rust in adverse conditions. To prevent this, wipe them with a slightly oily rag when new. If damage has already been done, use metal polish for nickel to remove the rust before using the oily rag.

Xylophone bars will be damaged by prolonged exposure to direct sunlight. This has the effect of breaking the lacquer seal on the wood, which then loses some of its natural moisture. The pitch of the bar will then alter.

Store instruments away from radiators.

If the pitch of a bar is faulty, return it to the manufacturer for retuning.

If you lose a bar, and wish to order a replacement, state clearly to the manufacturer:
(a) for which instrument
(b) for which note (A, B, C, etc)
(c) for which octave (lower or higher)
(d) the approximate metric dimensions of the bar

THE BOX ITSELF

If a persistent buzz develops when a certain note or range of notes is played, it may be that the glue has dried out in the base of the offending resonance chamber (i.e. one of the sections into which the box is subdivided). The resultant air-leak may be closed by brushing a stout mix of Cascamite powder glue between the base and the four sides of the chamber. Allow it to dry for twelve hours before further use. For emergency repairs just before a concert, put a damp cloth into the box to expand the wood and temporarily heal the crack.

THE NATURE AND CHARACTERISTICS OF THE INSTRUMENTS

HOW TO GET STARTED

Children make much more rapid progress on tuned percussion if they have an opportunity to use them in break time, or in their spare moments. A music corner in an Infant School is a valuable asset, but it is equally important to let Juniors have access to instruments for practice.

If you have no tuned percussion whatsoever, you can nevertheless set up a group music-making ensemble consisting of	voices, descant recorders, a guitar, and untuned percussion. The first tuned percussion instruments to be bought might be CHIME BARS, particularly if the children are young.
If you want to develop pitched work and are not sure which tuned percussion instruments to buy first (supposing that you can afford more than a few chime bars)....	Choose a diatonic alto xylophone first: (a) Its pitch is comparable with that of a child's singing voice, and its timbre is particularly clear. (b) It is sufficiently low to accompany songs, and strong enough in tone to support a class singing. (c) It is just large enough to accommodate two children seated side by side.
and next?	In this order:- (a) a diatonic soprano xylophone (to extend the pitch range available and to give a fuller texture) (b) an alto glockenspiel (for contrast of timbre) (c) a soprano glockenspiel (to further extend the pitch range).
...and if money is no object?	(d) a soprano metallophone, (e) a bass xylophone, (f) a soprano metallophone, (g) a bass metallophone

A Note on Chime Bars

These consist of a resonating chamber (usually a small box, sometimes a tube) supporting a bar, usually of metal, but sometimes of wood. Each note is a separate instrument, and the range of pitches available is quite extensive. Where money is limited, there are advantages in being able to buy a few chime bars at a time, instead of having to wait for a larger instrument. The very smallest chime bars (about 8 cm. long) are poor, however. The first bars that should be purchased are G, A, B, D, E (see page 38).

THE NATURE AND CHARACTERISTICS OF THE INSTRUMENTS

SPECIAL EFFECTS

Typical tremolo notation

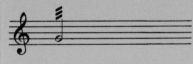

Alternative notation

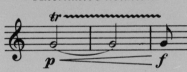

12. Tremolo

This is a roll, and is particularly effective on xylophones. Hold two beaters in one hand, separating them with the index finger. Twist them through ninety degrees so that the end of a bar of the instrument nearest to the player separates them, one above and one below. Strike the bar alternately from above and below, very slowly at first, but gradually increasing speed with practice. Aim for a smooth, regular roll.

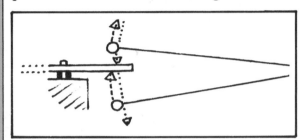

A tremolo can also be produced by striking the bars in the normal way, from above, alternately using the right and the left hand beater. Much practice is necessary to achieve a smooth roll.

A kind of tremolo can be made by pulling the ridged plastic handle of a beater slowly over the uppermost corner of a glockenspiel or metallophone bar at the end nearest the player. It is possible, with practice, to play a 'tremolo melody' in this way, pulling the handle over the edge of each successive bar in turn.

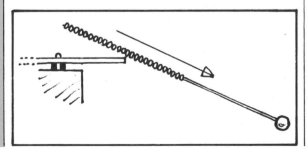

13. Glissando

Without exerting downward pressure, draw the head of the beater over the bars of the instrument from right to left or *vice versa*, depending on whether a downward or upward glissando is required. See below.

Sometimes it is necessary to sound the note at the end of the glissando distinctly: in this case, strike it with the beater in the other hand.

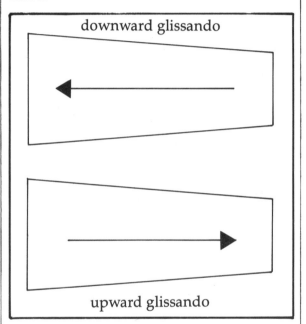

downward glissando

upward glissando

14. Unusual Timbre

This is often useful in atmospheric or descriptive music. Try striking the side of the resonance box of one of the larger instruments rhythmically with a hard beater. Another way of producing an unusual tone-colour is to strike the bars of a metallophone with the long edge of one of its own bars: this also works with a glockenspiel. (Never strike the bars of a xylophone with a metal bar). These are only two of many possibilities, of course.

PART TWO: Early Work with Tuned Percussion

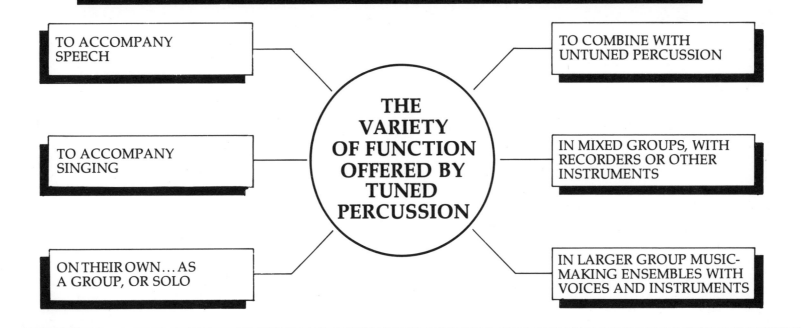

TO ACCOMPANY SPEECH

TO ACCOMPANY SINGING

ON THEIR OWN... AS A GROUP, OR SOLO

THE VARIETY OF FUNCTION OFFERED BY TUNED PERCUSSION

TO COMBINE WITH UNTUNED PERCUSSION

IN MIXED GROUPS, WITH RECORDERS OR OTHER INSTRUMENTS

IN LARGER GROUP MUSIC-MAKING ENSEMBLES WITH VOICES AND INSTRUMENTS

TUNED PERCUSSION TO ACCOMPANY SPEECH

1. A DRONE (See page 14) is an effective basic accompaniment to speech:

(Repeated continuously as an accompaniment)

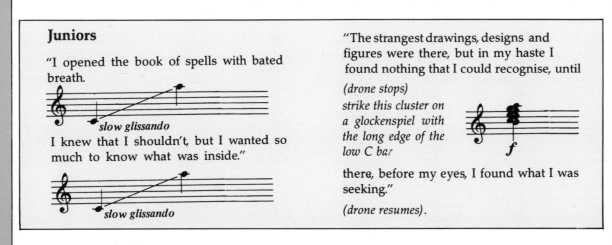

Juniors

"I opened the book of spells with bated breath.

slow glissando

I knew that I shouldn't, but I wanted so much to know what was inside."

slow glissando

"The strangest drawings, designs and figures were there, but in my haste I found nothing that I could recognise, until

(drone stops)

strike this cluster on a glockenspiel with the long edge of the low C bar

f

there, before my eyes, I found what I was seeking."

(drone resumes).

This example uses MUSICAL EFFECTS (see page 10) to heighten the atmosphere of the narrative, but repetitive phrases can be equally effective:

slowly

glockenspiel

TUNED PERCUSSION TO ACCOMPANY SPEECH

Ideas for developing the game

Repeat the game with two more verses:

"One little......ten little owlies"
(ending in "Whoo-hoo")
"Ten little......one little owlie."
(ending in "Boo" as before)

and

"One litle......ten little black cats"
(ending in "Meeow, meeow")
"Ten little......one little black cat."
(ending in"Boo" as before)

Choose other instruments and/or other notes for verses 2 and 3

For a cumulative effect let both instruments (in verse 2) and all three (in verse 3) play together after "Ten little....." (the fourth line)

An alternative note pattern
(more difficult)

If you try this, follow it with a listening game if the instruments are sufficiently differentiated in sound.....
"Who is this, the witch, the owlie or the cat?"
(teacher strikes one of the three instruments)

2. Use an appropriate sound (or sounds) to comment musically on verse or narrative. An example is given for a game with young Infants. Adapt the verbal material to suit juniors, possibly using a wider range of notes on the instrument(s).

Infants

One little, two little, three little witches,

four little, five little, six little witches,

Seven little, eight little, nine little witches,

Ten little Halloween witches!

Ten little, nine little, eight little witches

Seven little, six little, five little witches,

Four little, three little, two little witches

One little Halloween witch

◆ (while everyone shouts "Hee, Heeee, Hee, Heeee")

◆◆ (followed immediately by a loud shout of "Boo!")

Choose any two notes of contrasting pitch for this game

Use whatever tuned percussion is available

Always look for ideas to develop a singing game, and try to let it lead to a listening game, for aural training is of fundamental importance in music teaching.

As this is a COUNTING CHANT, it may be used as a finger play in which children try to show the appropriate number of fingers, rising then falling.

This game teaches SENSITIVITY TO DYNAMIC CONTRAST (three quiet notes followed by a group of loud notes)

It also teaches PITCH DISCRIMINATION (Use the words *"High* C" and *"Low* C")

The listening game teaches DISCRIMINATION OF TIMBRE

PERCUSSION INSTRUMENTS TO ACCOMPANY SINGING

INFANTS

3. It is a small step from choral speaking to vocal chanting. Children chant spontaneously using a 'sing-song' voice, and this very primitive form of singing is used in the scene which is outlined below. The falling minor third (G—E in this example, but it could be F—D, or any other pairs of notes in the *soh—me* relationship) is a natural mode of expression at a very early age; it is therefore sensible to use it in the Infant School.

ACCOMPANYING CHANTS

Infants

The prince lies in a glade in a forest, apparently dead. The narrator (a child) invokes all available forces, natural and unnatural, to attempt to revive him......

Narrator's continuous incantation:

Sun-beams come,   Sun-beams come

Drone accompaniment (continues throughout)

The sunbeams, suitably dressed in yellow, dance around the prince, extending their arms in curving movements over his face. As they do so, a high chime bar is struck twice:

they retire

Narrator:

Wi - zard come,   Wi - zard come

The wizard, wearing a long cloak, enters and cautiously circles the prostrate prince. He waves a wand, and, as he does so, a beater is quickly drawn across the middle bars of a glockenspiel, to and fro:

(*he withdraws*)

Narrator:

Wind   come,   Wind   come

The wind, wearing a cloak of very thin material, alternately gathers speed and slows down, the garment billowing with his sudden movements. He wafts the air around the prince's face repeatedly, but with no effect. As he does so, one note is struck repeatedly:

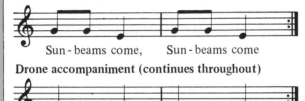

The drone for both pieces.

● Note that the narrator's falling minor third is typical of a young child's spontaneous chanting which occurs naturally when he is at play.

● Note the scope here for the use of music, drama and dance on an equal footing.

PERCUSSION INSTRUMENTS TO ACCOMPANY SINGING

DRONE ACCOMPANIMENTS

A basic accompaniment such as that provided on folk instruments like the Appalachian Dulcimer or bagpipes is most suitable to accompany this elemental chanting. Such instruments have one or two notes sounding continuously, an accompaniment which is called a DRONE. The natural drone to accompany a G—E chant is an open fifth,

C—G:

As it tends to function as the bass of the texture it is usually assigned to the lowest tuned instrument available. Make sure that C is the *lower* of the two notes on the instruments, otherwise an unstable interval

of a fourth will result:

 incorrect drone

The drone may be played as written, with the two notes sounding simultaneously, or they may be separated:

There is much scope for variety, for these separated notes may be played steadily (as a pulse) or made more rhythmically interesting:

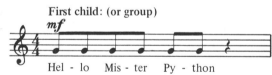

Let the drone start the piece, and become stable before the singers begin. It often continues uninterrupted, through a section.

"The Python" by Spike Milligan

Note the DYNAMICS suggested in this piece

mf moderately loud
p quiet
f loud

ALWAYS be aware of the huge difference dynamics can make to the quality of music

JUNIORS

The same musical material is used with Juniors who are new to this work, though the words used should be suitable. In the example below the chant notes G—E do not alternate regularly throughout as they did in the Infant piece, neither does the drone play continually. The vocal line is shared between two parts; this division of labour, which is a change from constant whole-class singing, helps maintain interest.

Instead of accompanying throughout, as in the piece for Infants, the drone merely interjects comments at the ends of phrases....yet it is still an accompaniment to the chanting. Instead of alternating E and G throughout, the vocal line begins on G alone: only in the second part is E introduced.

PART THREE: Transfer of Ideas from Untuned to Tuned Percussion

Work on tuned percussion is built upon a firm rhythmic training.

1. As far as possible, treat work on tuned percussion instruments as an extension of purely rhythmic work using
(a) body percussion sounds (CLAPPING, KNEE-SLAPPING, STAMPING and FINGER-SNAPS)
(b) untuned percussion.

The first technique in rhythm training is IMITATION (echoing), a process by means of which children acquire a basic *practical* rhythmic vocabulary. With the youngest children, begin with nonsense echoes. Try to incorporate contrasts of mood, speed, pitch and dynamics.

Nonsense Echoes:
Nursery/Infant

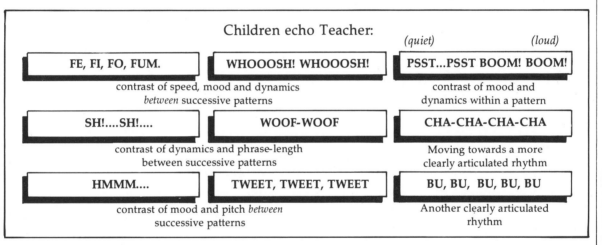

Children echo Teacher:

| | | (quiet) | (loud) |

| FE, FI, FO, FUM. | WHOOOSH! WHOOOSH! | PSST...PSST BOOM! BOOM! |
| contrast of speed, mood and dynamics *between* successive patterns | | contrast of mood and dynamics within a pattern |

| SH!....SH!.... | WOOF-WOOF | CHA-CHA-CHA-CHA |
| contrast of dynamics and phrase-length between successive patterns | | Moving towards a more clearly articulated rhythm |

| HMMM.... | TWEET, TWEET, TWEET | BU, BU, BU, BU, BU |
| contrast of mood and pitch *between* successive patterns | | Another clearly articulated rhythm |

Rhythmic Echoes:
Infants

2a. Middle infants enjoy the same game, but are also perfectly capable of echoing phrases clapped and spoken by the teacher.

◆ In the early stages, begin on a strong beat

◆◆ leave a 'breathing space' to give the children a chance

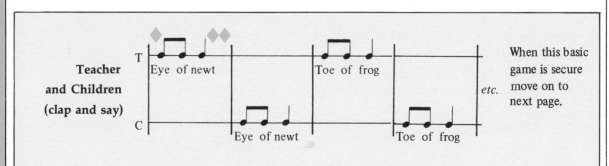

Teacher and Children (clap and say)

T — Eye of newt — Toe of frog — *etc.*

C — Eye of newt — Toe of frog

When this basic game is secure move on to next page.

Rhythmic Echoes: Juniors	**2b.** To extend the game, and expose the rhythm more clearly, the teacher can repeat each item, but without speaking the rhythm the second time (see below). The children will probably continue to think the words while clapping the rhythms, and the verbal material will remain a valuable means to an end.

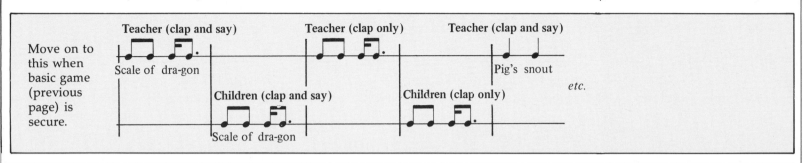

Singing Echoes: Juniors	**3.** Sing the echo game using only one or two notes. Use the same words as in 2 above.

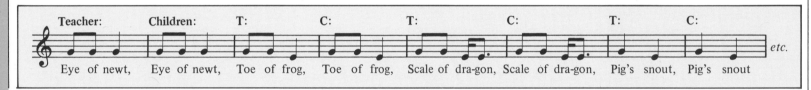

A Singing Game	**4.** When the children are secure, invent singing games using only two notes. In the game which is illustrated, the class sings the chorus after which a volunteer offers something for the cauldron.

Some possible drone patterns: (any tuned percussion instrument—preferably a xylophone)	**5.** A C—G drone will add an element of continuity to these games. The exact nature of the drone may be left to the child. You might 'reward' the soloist who has just offered something for the cauldron by letting him provide the drone accompaniment for the next chorus.
Theme for Junior Work: Ingredients for the Witch's Cauldron	

Another two-note singing game

Teacher (pointing at cupboard):

Child (or Children:)

I spy, with my lit - tle eye, Some-thing be - gin - ning with "C"

cup - board!

Ideas for development of this game:
Repeat with various objects in the room
Let children take the teacher's part when they are confident

Tuned percussion or recorders may accompany or echo the teacher's question and/or echo the child's answer
(This fosters keen listening — important in every music lesson.)

More Two-note Chants

Don't forget to accompany the game and the chants with two-note drones.

Competition for the best alternative words? Everyone sings (then plays) his contribution.

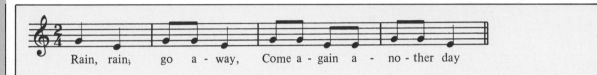

Rain, rain, go a - way, Come a - gain a - no - ther day

After singing this, let a xylophone play bars 1-2 and recorders 3-4, then vice-versa

Ro - ses are red, Vi - o - lets are blue; Su - gar is sweet and so are you

Now try this expansion of "I spy....."

Add a drone. Agree in advance exactly where it will play each time.

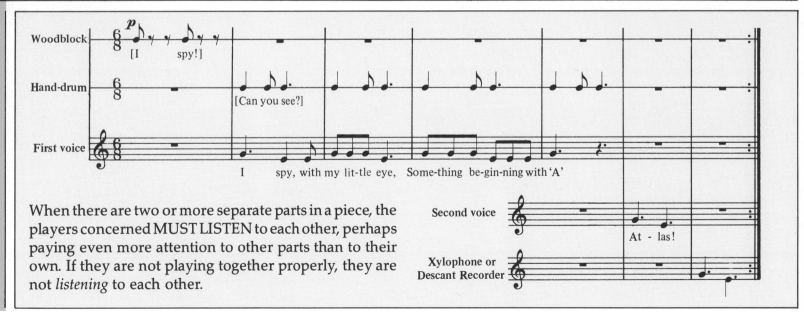

Woodblock

[I spy!]

Hand-drum

[Can you see?]

First voice

I spy, with my lit - tle eye, Some-thing be - gin - ning with 'A'

When there are two or more separate parts in a piece, the players concerned MUST LISTEN to each other, perhaps paying even more attention to other parts than to their own. If they are not playing together properly, they are not *listening* to each other.

Second voice

At - las!

Xylophone or Descant Recorder

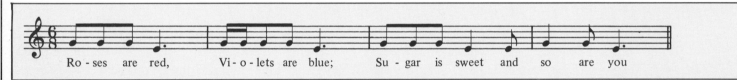

THE BEGINNINGS OF IMPROVISATION ON TUNED PERCUSSION

PHRASE-RESPONSE PATTERNS

Use a phrase/response framework but *begin* with body-percussion sounds and untuned percussion, so that children get the idea first.

Rhythmic phrases and responses as an introduction to improvisation

* Possible comments on children's response to clapped rhythms.

6. Purpose: to encourage a feeling for phrase-rhythms

(a) When their rhythmic vocabulary becomes more secure through echo games, encourage children to give you back a *different* rhythm instead of repeating yours. This is sometimes called "question and answer", but this description is a bit of a misnomer, because children do not always think of what they are doing as an answer. In "Music for Children", Book I (Schott), Orff used the description "Rhythms to be completed", a sort of "your turn .... my turn" game. It is a phrase/response idea offering a framework for the earliest attempts at improvisation.

(b) Make the phrase/response idea into a more continuous piece (as different pairs contribute in turn) by adding an underlying pulse or ostinato on a different instrument from anyone else's.

(c) Comment from time to time, even if it means interrupting the flow. Some examples of possible comments are given below. It would be counterproductive to interrupt the flow too often; you might hear four pairs of phrases before commenting. As the children become more experienced, encourage them to comment on their own contributions, and on those of others.

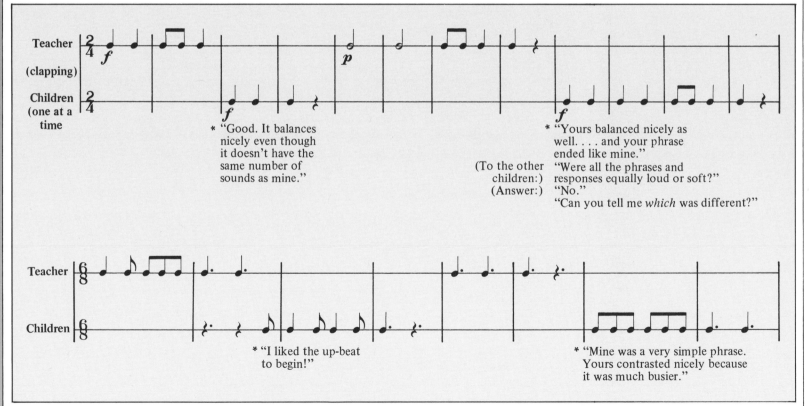

Teacher (clapping)

Children (one at a time

* "Good. It balances nicely even though it doesn't have the same number of sounds as mine."

* "Yours balanced nicely as well. . . . and your phrase ended like mine."

(To the other children:) "Were all the phrases and responses equally loud or soft?"
(Answer:) "No."
"Can you tell me *which* was different?"

Teacher

Children

* "I liked the up-beat to begin!"

* "Mine was a very simple phrase. Yours contrasted nicely because it was much busier."

Note the importance of ASKING QUESTIONS to underline the value of LISTENING

BE POSITIVE, and try to reinforce something of value in each responding phrase

THE BEGINNINGS OF IMPROVISATION ON TUNED PERCUSSION

Mixed Body-percussion

◆ Down-stems: left hand on left knee

Up-stems: right hand on right knee

(d) Begin with teacher-child phrases and responses, but aim to have the children working in pairs as soon as possible. The first phrases can be clapped, but proceed to mixed body-percussion sounds, and then use untuned percussion.

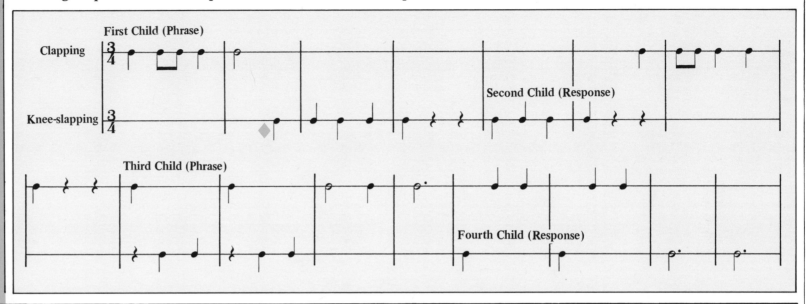

(e) Do not be concerned if some children find this difficult at first. Sometimes a response will not seem to relate to the phrase which preceded it, but gradually those who are having trouble will pick up ideas from the others. Remember also that in music the phrases do not always balance. A four-bar phrase MAY sometimes be followed perfectly satisfactorily by an eight-bar phrase, or one two bars long.

* Possible comments on children's response to clapped rhythms.

* "Your reply was much longer, but it certainly worked well."

TRANSFER THE PHRASE/RESPONSE FRAMEWORK FROM UNTUNED TO TUNED PERCUSSION.

Examples of phrase/response patterns on tuned percussion and voices

Some children prefer giving an answer on an instrument, others prefer singing an answer.

The singer has the advantage of the verbal rhythm if he can overcome his diffidence!

(Each of the respondents is given time beforehand to consider what he or she will offer for the cauldron....)

◆ An upbeat tends to occur spontaneously in this context.

◆◆ drone accompaniment?

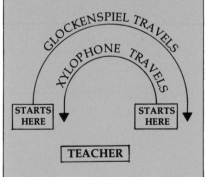

Classroom organisation of tuned percussion work

7.

Whereas in rhythmic work echo precedes the phrase/response framework (page 18, 6a), in melodic work children may find it easier to reply to a phrase on a tuned percussion instrument than to echo it. Begin with a very restricted range of notes, adding one at a time as the children improve.

Phrase = P   Response = R

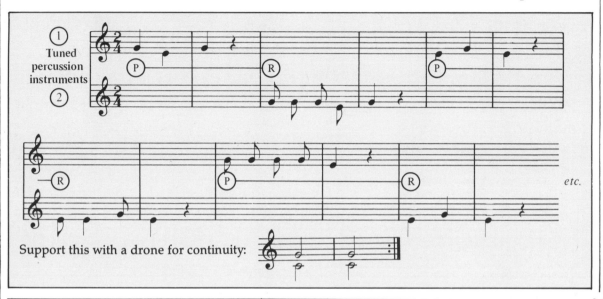

Support this with a drone for continuity:

8. "Ingredients for the Brew" is an example of a vocal phrase/response game.

9. Arrange the children in two concentric semicircles, and give the child on one end of each a tuned percussion instrument with all its bars removed except those you intend using (G and E at this stage). When the first child in the outer semicircle has played a phrase in reponse to yours, he passes his instrument to his neighbour. Meanwhile the child on the other end of the inner semicircle listens to your next phrase, responds, and then passes his instrument to his neighbour. So the game proceeds. Note the following:-

(a) The teacher avoids phrases like ♫ ♫ which give the next child insufficient time to consider his reponse. Leave a "breathing space", both in echo work and here.

TRANSFER THE PHRASE/RESPONSE FRAMEWORK FROM UNTUNED TO TUNED PERCUSSION.

(b) It takes very little time to play this game, and it gives everyone a chance to play on an instrument; this is not always possible in a lesson!

(c) A C—G drone throughout will contribute a sense of flow and make for continuity.

8 on page 20 relies on words for the rhythmic shape of the melodic (vocal) responses. 2b on page 16 illustrates the gradual withdrawal of words as audible articulations of rhythms. Here, in 9, a melodic phrase/response framework without the support of words paves the way for increasing independence.

◆ It might be appropriate to interrupt for a moment to comment favourably on the glockenspiel's last phrase which inverted the teacher's phrase, and the xylophone's response, which included an up-beat. Such reinforcement gives others ideas.

(e) Reinforce sensitivity to the individual capabilities of instruments by means of favourable comment (e.g. slow, sustained notes on a metallophone, or quick, running phrases on a xylophone).

Drone accompaniment?

MORE IDEAS FOR RHYTHMIC ECHO-GAMES, LEADING TO THE IMPROVISATION OF A RONDO

In order to improve facility on melodic percussion, continually strengthen the rhythm.

10. A secure sense of rhythm is a fundamental prerequisite for facility and improvement in tuned percussion work. Continue to introduce rhythmic games alongside melodic work. The following are developments of the rhythmic echoing introduced on pages 15 and 16.

(a) Dispense with words completely, and gradually increase the child's rhythmic vocabulary (e.g. use of triplets)

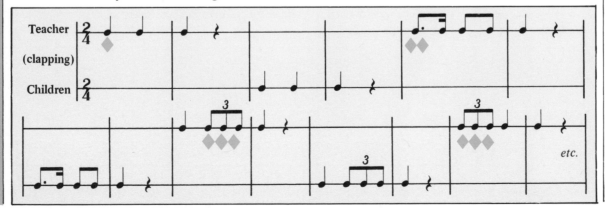

◆ dispense with words.

◆◆ introduce more interesting rhythms.

◆◆◆ introduce a triplet...... but reinforce it

MORE IDEAS FOR RHYTHMIC ECHO-GAMES, LEADING TO THE IMPROVISATION OF A RONDO

In bar 2, the teacher counts "—2 3" aloud to help the children enter accurately.

Body percussion echoes

(b) Introduce up-beats and syncopation without comment. These rarely cause problems in echo work.

(c) Vary the metre. Do not restrict yourself to 2/4, but use 3/4, 4/4 and 6/8 on various occasions.

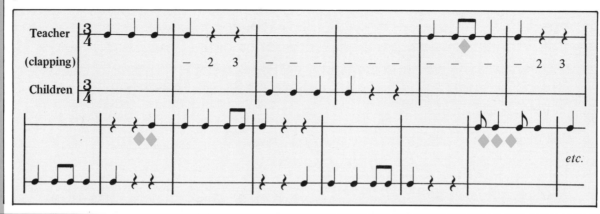

◆ 'Split' each of the whole notes in turn in successive phrases

◆◆ Introduce the up-beat spontaneously

◆◆◆ Introduce syncopation

This is an artificial exercise, in that too many new elements are introduced in quick succession. Each needs reinforcement.

(d) Use various body-percussion sounds in combination.

(e) Encourage awareness of dynamics by giving quiet phrases, loud phrases, crescendo and decrescendo passages.

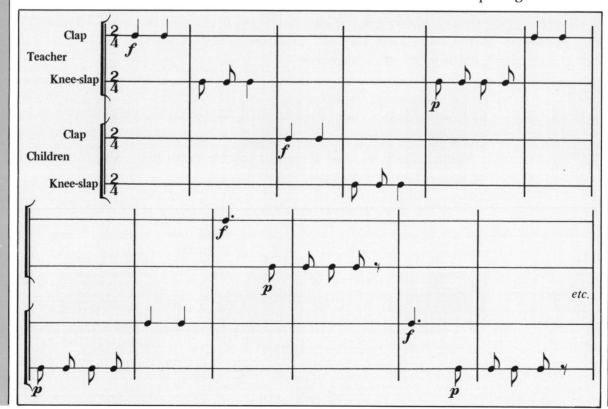

This game develops co-ordination, offers a contrast of TIMBRE, and leads to an increased awareness of dynamics

MORE IDEAS FOR RHYTHMIC ECHO-GAMES, LEADING TO THE IMPROVISATION OF A RONDO

Reversed Dynamics

(f) Play "reversed dynamics", in which the children echo your rhythm, but with the opposite dynamic.

Note the preoccupation with DYNAMICS

Double Echoes

◆ Teacher counts...2, and brings in ① with a firm down-beat

◆◆ Teacher counts....2, and brings in ① and ② together.

◆◆◆ Gives an opportunity for two rhythms to sound together.

(g) Play "double echoes" Divide the class into two parts, ① and ②

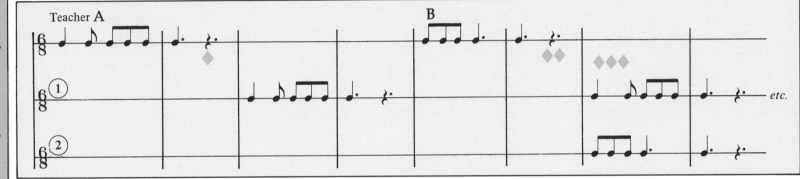

● Teacher claps A ● ① echoes A ● Teachers claps B ● ① re-echoes A, and at the same time ● ② echoes B

◆ Teaches children to count accurately through silent bars

(h) Play "memory echoes" Divide the class into two parts, ① and ②

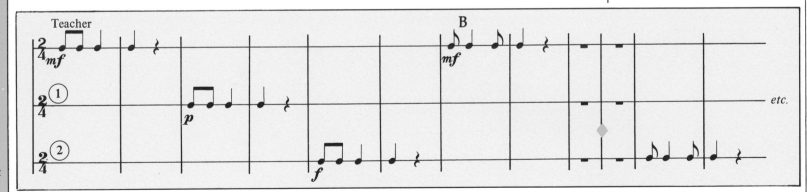

● Teacher claps A mf
● ① echoes A p
● ② re-echoes A f

● Teacher claps B mf
◆ ① thinks the rhythm of B silently to see if ② comes in on time.

● ② echoes B f (after leaving a big enough gap for A to have echoed)

THE IMPROVISATION OF A RONDO

Echo Rondo

(i) Improvise a RONDO

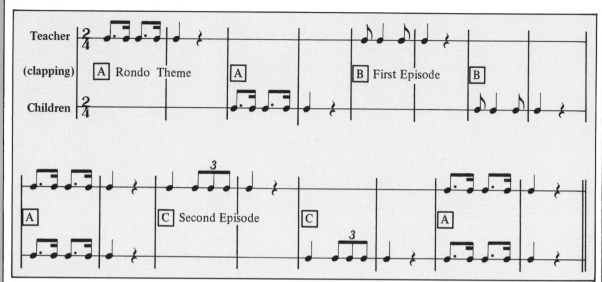

- Teacher claps A
- Children echo A
- Teacher claps B
- Children echo B
- All clap A
- Teacher claps C
- Children echo C
- All clap A

This shows the importance of FORMAL frameworks and teaches the children what a RONDO is.

In a RONDO, the "main theme" (A) keeps coming around, separated in its appearances by contrasting EPISODES (B, C).

PREPARATIONS FOR ECHO WORK ON TUNED PERCUSSION

Singing Games

11. The stages leading to echo work on tuned percussion instruments are as follows:

(a) Singing games in which children echo the teacher. This is traditionally the way in which many children learn a new song; they should not, therefore, find anything unusual in such games, except, perhaps, the restricted range of notes to begin. The restriction does, however, facilitate early work in pairs where ① sings a phrase to "la" and ② echoes it. At the earliest stage, do not place too much emphasis on accuracy of pitch, even if it is one of the ultimate aims of the exercise, but encourage willingness to take part, and try to foster enjoyment.

A singing game — vocal echoes using E and G only.

As in rhythm games, introduce the up-beat without comment

PREPARATIONS FOR ECHO WORK ON TUNED PERCUSSION

A vocal RONDO for Infants

Development idea: Let someone play the RONDO theme on one tuned percussion instrument, or on chime bars, and someone else repeat the episodes on another.

The whole was accompanied by the simple drone:
(Alto Xylophone)

(b) The linking of these short vocal phrases into a larger form. "Market Stall", was improvised by six-year-olds, who accompanied it throughout by means of a simple drone: it is a tiny vocal rondo. Infants delight in suggesting what they might sell in an imaginary shop! Play the same game on different occasions, changing the type of shop each time. Relate the game to a story for greater effect.

The main aim on this page is to improve children's perception of PITCH and thus prepare them for echo games on TUNED PERCUSSION

Echo work with recorders

Keep repeating phrases using only B, but varying the rhythm until you feel the children are ready to go on to A.

(c) Echo work on recorders. Use only the notes B, A and G to begin with. For further developments of this idea, see pages 38 and 39. As soon as instruments are used, the finding and producing of a note have to be considered, a slower process than singing, which many children find almost instinctive. Therefore begin with only one note, and alter the rhythm of each phrase given for echoing. Then progess to two, and then three notes. At first, children will watch your fingers rather than listen to the note: there is no objection to this, for the eye should aid the ear. When they are more secure, turn away from them, thus removing the visual aid.

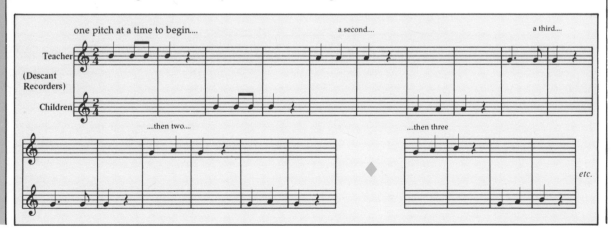

◆ more phrases using two notes before continuing.

ECHO WORK ON TUNED PERCUSSION

Echo one of these four phrases on tuned percussion

Try these echo games using the concentric semicircles organisation (page 20).

◆ Children use appropriate hand-signs if you wish

12. The games and exercises on the previous pages have been kept deliberately simple. Children find echo games on tuned percussion instruments quite challenging; it is therefore important to continue this approach, and simplify the task as much as possible, in order to increase the chances of initial success. Many Secondary School children fear Aural Training because the early tasks given to them were too difficult. The following restrictions are designed to contribute to the young child's chance of early success:

(a) Agree on a constant rhythm (say ♩ ♩ | ♩ 𝄽 ‖

(b) Continue to use only two notes — G and E

(c) Agree that, to begin with, the first note will be G. There are only four possibilities. (See below). The fourth is only possible if it is agreed that one may use only one of the two notes sometimes.

(d) The first child, ① plays one of the four possibilities, and ② echoes him.

(e) The whole class may sing ①'s phrase to "la" before ② echoes. [If this activity is too slight for the children, their singing may be accompanied by the appropriate hand-signs. (See Margaret O'Shea's book in this series). Alternatively, or additionally, solfa syllables may be sung].

la, la, la
(or: soh, soh, me)

la, la, la
(or soh, me, soh)

(f) Accompany the process with a C—G drone)

a drone pattern for continuity

*ECHO WORK ON
TUNED PERCUSSION*

(g) When this is all secure, agree that henceforth the first note is E instead of G

The four possibilites when the first note is E

(h) When this is secure, increase the difficulty by agreeing that the first note may be E *or* G.

(i) Then agree to substitute two quavers for the first or second crotchet.

The increased range of possibilites when the first note is E or G, and when two quavers are substituted for one of the first two crotchets How can you develop this idea further?

---

13. The use of the notes G and E has been emphasised, and it is assumed that the children are ready for a third note. By this stage they will KNOW the notes G and E in terms of (a) playing them on tuned percussion

(b) singing them accurately
(c) differentiating between them aurally
(d) reading them by means of traditional notation
(e) using them for improvisation

Add the note A to G and E for improvisation

14 The third 'melody note' is A. (C is also available, but only in a drone as yet). The note A comes naturally to children; they use it in playground games. It is so spontaneous that they find the combination of A—G—E easier than any other group of three notes for improvisation.

La, la, la, la, la,___ la ___

Children's spontaneous playground chant

ECHO WORK ON
TUNED PERCUSSION

◆ See ◆ on page 34

Ask the children

See if children can continue the verse, supplying an answer to A. A. Milne's question. Try setting the best answer to the G—A—G—E note pattern. This is the actual conclusion of the poem:

*I sometimes call him Terrible John,
'cos his tail goes on—
And on—
and on—
I sometimes call him Terrible Jack,
'Cos his tail goes on to the end of his back.
And I sometimes call him Terrible James,
'Cos he says he likes me calling him names
But I think I shall call him Jim,
'Cos I am fond of him.*

15. Sing many songs using A—G—E. A particularly useful pattern as a basis for improvisation is G—A—G—E. If this pattern is repeated, it can be used to set a rhyme or verse. Figure A is a primitive setting in that its second, third and fourth phrases are identical rhythmically and melodically, but it is this repetition which contributes to rapid learning, and therefore allows early playing on tuned percussion; it also gives a basic idea which enhances the possibility of improvisation. Although Figure B uses the same melodic structure, it is more interesting because of the rhythmic contrasts in the second and fourth phrases.

16. Accompany these songs with decorated drones. C and G remain the two basic notes, but G is decorated by A.

A decorated drone

Examples of C—G drones using A as a decorative note

EXPANDING A MELODY AND ACCOMPANIMENT INTO A TERNARY PIECE

◆ The singers and alto glockenspiel come in immediately after they have heard "my poor little dormouse" twice from the body-percussion group

◆◆ These two G's are given by a chime bar, recorder, and any tuned percussion for the benefit of the singers: they coincide with the second two claps.

◆◆◆ It is often effective to mark the end of a phrase (particularly if there is a rest) in this way.

◆◆◆◆ Melodic accompaniments stop to allow the drum to make an impact.

17. Up to now the main accompaniment to singing has been a drone on a tuned percussion instrument. If you have two such instruments, or one and a set of chime bars, you can add a second accompaniment strand. This melodic ostinato uses the same notes as the melody, but in a different order.

straight on to the B section

Section B *on the following page.*

EXPANDING A MELODY AND ACCOMPANIMENT INTO A TERNARY PIECE

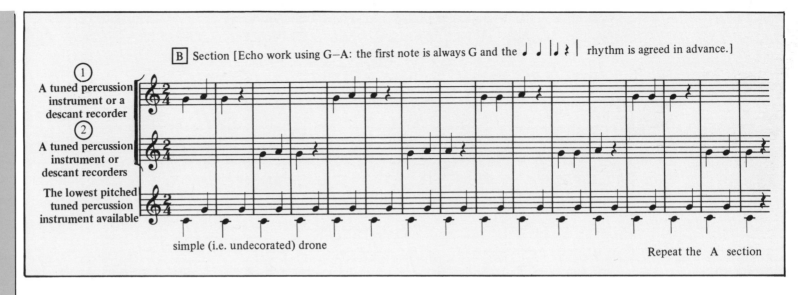

Look at the alto glockenspiel part on the previous page. It is obviously derived from the melody, but differs slightly from it. An accompanying melodic ostinato may be quite different in rhythm and shape from the melody: this is where discretion has to be exercised—on your part as an adviser and on the child's as an improviser. If children find it difficult to improvise such a pattern, let them base it on words from (or derived from) the song. The alto glockenspiel ostinato might have been based on "but his tail is big".

Echo work can now include the note A: begin by using a pair of notes (A—G or G—A) as before (page 26), but quickly progress to the stage when the phrase to be echoed can begin on A, G or E and include any of the following pairs of notes: A—G, G—A, G—E, E—G. A—E is left until last as the leap proves more difficult to echo.

Expand a melody and accompaniment into a Ternary Form piece (ABA), as above. Here there is a body-percussion pattern as an introduction followed by the setting of the words using the G—A—G—E pattern and accompanied by a decorated drone and a melodic ostinato. The 'B' section consists of melodic echo work using the notes G and A only, always starting with G.

ADDING THE NOTE D TO G, A AND E FOR IMPROVISATION

Incantation to two orange pips on the hearth (Trad).

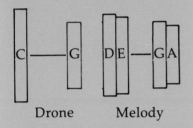

Play the melodies on tuned percussion over the drones given at the beginning of each.

Then make each into a ternary piece:

A singing
B playing ⎤ The melody
A singing ⎦

▼ Important notes in each phrase tend to be drone notes, or to be particularly consonant with them

Ideas for further developments

(a) add an ostinato part to each melody using D, E, G, A.

(b) try decorating the drones. Decorate one of the drone's notes by using an adjacent note

(c) Extend the pieces by adding an Introduction and or Coda (tailpiece): these can consist of the drone, or accompanying ostinato, or both

18. So far, the notes used for improvising melodies have been limited to A, G and E: C has also been available as one of the two drone notes.

The addition of a fourth note —D not only increases the scope of improvisation, but also extends the number of drones available. Although it was not pointed out earlier, as soon as the note A was introduced, the drone A—E became available:

DRONE
A — E

ANOTHER IDEA FOR A TERNARY-FORM PIECE

Try improvising a new "B" section to the music on page 29 using the A—E drone instead of C—G, changing back to C—G for the return of the "A" section. The effect is as if the middle section of the piece were in the minor key, contrasting with the more major-sounding "A" sections.

When D is added to the notes for improvisation, the number of drones is increased to four:

The choice of drone now determines the nature of the melody to some extent. In the example on the previous page there are four settings of the same words, each using the same rhythm. Try each melody with each of the four drones in turn, and you will see that one seems to 'fit' better than the others: this is because it conditioned the shape of the melody in the first place.

◆ Begin with this
◆◆ Available when A is added to the notes for improvisation
◆◆◆ Not available until D is added as well.

INTRODUCING EXTENDED DRONES . . . TO ACCOMPANY PHRASES AND RESPONSES USING D, E, G AND A

19. After further experience of echo-work and phrase/response patterns on untuned percussion, children should be acquiring a larger rhythmic vocabulary which they can use in further phrase/response patterns on tuned percussion using D, E, G and A. Let voices, recorders and even orchestral instruments, if available, join in at this stage: the only constraint is the small number of notes which are being used at the time, and which offer a slightly greater problem to a recorder player or violinist than to a child playing a xylophone, who is able to remove all the bars except for those on which he is improvising. Examples of this work follow here and on page 33.

phrase = (P) response = (R)

Notice the difference in mood between this piece and the one on page 33. It is largely the result of the contrast between the C—G and the A—E drone.

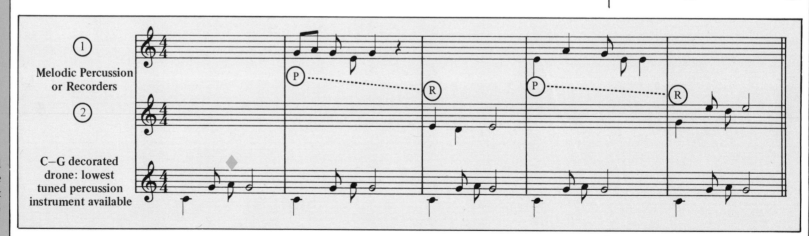

◆ The upper drone note G is decorated by A

INTRODUCING EXTENDED DRONES . . . TO ACCOMPANY PHRASES AND RESPONSES USING D, E, G AND A

As before, a drone will tend to unify the exercise, transforming it into a continuous piece. If a C—G drone is used on the first occasion, a D—A drone might be tried next time, and, subsequently, G—D and A—E. Notice the subtle difference in the overall sound of the texture each time the drone is changed. Use decorated drones frequently: the less able, of course, can continue to use a simple drone. In this work, each child may contribute at his own level.

When children are familiar with decorated drones, extended drones may be introduced to add further variety. An extension of a drone simply involves the doubling of one of its two notes (or perhaps both) at the octave.

Some examples of EXTENDED drones

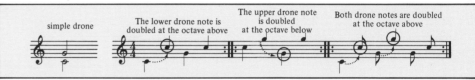

In the example below the phrase/response pattern is accompanied by an extended drone.

The first two notes form the basic drone, so the upper drone note is doubled at the octave below

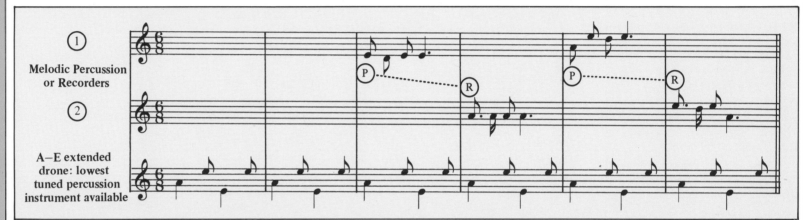

SUGGESTIONS FOR IMPROVISING MUSIC USING THE NOTES D, E, G AND A

Incorporate untuned instruments into musical textures even though the emphasis is on tuned percussion. Vary their function.

20. Try expanding the melodies on page 31 into ABA pieces. On page 34 is a pattern for such expansion. In the "B" section, the C—G drone used in the "A" section is exchanged for D—A to support a melodic phrase/response pattern, and the xylophone's ostinato is dropped. It might have been retained, or another substituted: decide in each case to what extent the suggested pattern should be followed.

Decide on an effective untuned percussion accompaniment. Perhaps the "B" section could be devoted to rhythmic rather than melodic material.

Untuned percussion instruments might also be used:
(a) for an introduction
(b) for an interlude between the main sections A ▽ B ▽ A
(c) for a coda to round off the piece

▽ possibility of a rhythmic section as an interlude

Suggestions for improvising music using the notes D, E, G and A

◆ Filling in a rest in the melody in this way is often useful
(a) it may help to improve the rhythmic performance
(b) it gives the drummer a point of reference for each of his notes

◆◆ This ostinato stops for the [B] section

● Accompanying instruments ignore the up-beat, entering on the first main beat instead. Alternatively, the xylophone and metallophone may provide an introduction by beginning this accompaniment in the bar in which the voices enter on the last beat.

◆◆◆ change of drone from C—G to D—A

Decorated drone: A is decorated by means of G

Followed by a repeat of the A section

PART FOUR: The Pentatonic Scale

1. Add C to the four notes already used for improvisation to complete the pentatonic scale called C Pentatonic.

Why is the PENTATONIC SCALE popular in music teaching?

Although this note has been available from the beginning as a drone note, it is not used for improvisation until this stage on account of its magnetic effect. Once it has been introduced, it tends to be used as the last (and, to a lesser extent, the first) note of a melody to the exclusion of other notes. While there is nothing wrong with finishing a melody in C pentatonic on the note C, it is a pity if the other notes are never used for this purpose.

The pentatonic scale is chosen for the early stages of improvisation because it lacks the fourth and seventh notes of the major scale; there is a semitone between each of these notes and one of its neighbours, an interval which has the effect of attracting the fourth and seventh notes to the third and eighth respectively. In C major, B tends to be followed by C, and F by E. Because semitones are absent in the pentatonic scale, there is no such 'pull': neither is there a feeling of discord, whatever notes are sounded together in a pentatonic texture. Children may therefore combine improvised pentatonic melodies without harmonic constraints.

In order to encourage vocal improvisation, practise singing this scale to 'la' (a, b). Several singing games, based upon it, follow (c, d, e, f). Add drones and ostinato patterns on tuned percussion instruments (g).

Vary the time interval of the imitations: here the second part enters a semibreve after the first: try entering a minim later, or a dotted semibreve. Finally try adding a third vocal scale!

Pentatonic scales share with major and minor scales the possibility of starting on any note; however, with diatonic melodic percussion instruments, there are only five 'major' pentatonics and five 'minor'. (Illustrated right.)

The 'minor' pentatonics are merely versions of the scale which start on the penultimate note of the 'major' pentatonics. It is a useful distinction, for, combined with the drone on their first and fifth notes these minor pentatonics offer an opportunity of contrast within a piece.

The 'naming' note for each 'major' pentatonic is at the left hand end of a group of three notes ▽

The 'naming' note for each 'minor' pentatonic is the next note to the left of the 'naming' note for the appropriate 'major' pentatonic ▲

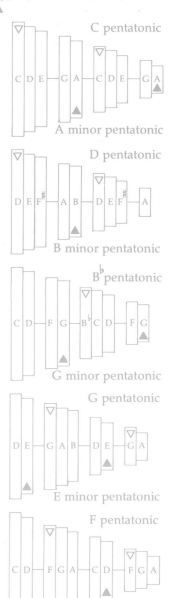

C pentatonic

A minor pentatonic

D pentatonic

B minor pentatonic

B♭ pentatonic

G minor pentatonic

G pentatonic

E minor pentatonic

F pentatonic

D minor pentatonic

THE PENTATONIC SCALE

Vocal Games using C pentatonic

When children have an opportunity to practise on tuned percussion in small groups, these imitation games accompanied by ostinato and drone patterns offer excellent material for the purpose

Try starting and ending on notes other than C. Are other drones more suitable in these cases?

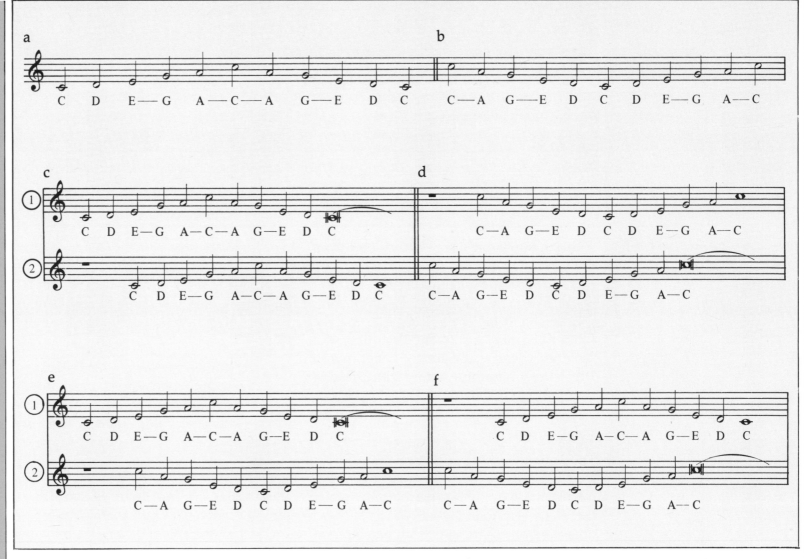

Instrumental Accompaniments to the Vocal Games

THE PENTATONIC SCALE

The palindrome (or cumulative ostinato)

This crescendo-decrescendo pattern is most useful to accompany, for example, a procession appearing on stage, celebrating an important event and then retiring.

An example of a palindrome ostinato using D pentatonic

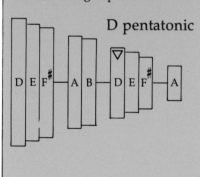

D pentatonic

2. A useful texture in dramatic situations which call for a sense of climax is the cumulative ostinato. If this texture is then reversed, forming a diminuendo, the two sections taken together form a palindrome ostinato. (See below).

(a) Choose a drone: it should be firm and rhythmic.
(b) Improvise pentatonic ostinato patterns on each of the other tuned percussion instruments available.
(c) When these are secure, and each child has decided what he is going to play, tell the children to enter one by one, but not until the previous child's playing is steady.
(d) As each child adds his ostinato to the texture there will be a feeling of climax.
(e) When all available tuned percussion are playing, a recorder player improvises, using the same pentatonic scale. When he stops, this marks where the instruments are withdrawn. Each stops playing in turn, beginning with the one which entered last before the recorder improvisation.
(f) As each instrument drops out, there is a gradual diminuendo, until only the drone is left. The child playing this finally stops in his own time.

Each bar will proably be repeated several times before the next instrument enters

The central ostinato bar is repeated eight times to accommodate the recorder improvisation

EXPLORING G PENTATONIC

How to Integrate Tuned Percussion and Recorders

If instruments are set up for C pentatonic, in order to change quickly to G pentatonic, say:
"Off with the C's....
On with the B's...."

3. Children learning to play the descant recorder begin with a restricted range of notes—probably G, A and B; even those who have progressed beyond this stage will benefit from beginning their improvisations with just a few notes.

G pentatonic, in that it contains the notes G, A and B, is a very useful scale from which to improvise an accompaniment to early recorder improvisations. Set up tuned percussion instruments with this scale.

(a) Begin with a drone, (simple, decorated or extended according to the level of ability of the child who is playing it) (see (a) in example on page 39.

(b) Add an ostinato accompaniment (when the drone is stable) (b).

(c) Give the recorder players *extremely* easy phrases to echo (c). If necessary, repeat even these easy phrases with other rhythms:

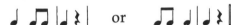

Subject each of the notes B, A and G to this repeated-note treatment before using two different notes in a phrase, and exhaust all the two-note possibilities before using all three in a phrase. You need not be so cautious as this, of course, if the children are quick to pick up the idea, but if they are very young, inexperienced recorder players, or in special education, err on the side of caution. To give other children in the class a task, let them sing the phrase you have played before the recorders re-echo.

(d) When you have given sufficient phrases in this way, change the drone (say to E-B). The same ostinato may continue, but you may wish to drop it or change it to vary the texture.

(e) Over the new accompaniment organise phrase/response patterns using B, A and G.

(f) Teach the Welsh folk-tune 'Suo-gân' by rote (see on page 39). Use it as a rondo theme (A section). Use the echo game and phrase/response patterns as episodes (B and C sections respectively). The same drone will serve for the A and B sections, but note the change of atmosphere in the C section when the drone shifts.

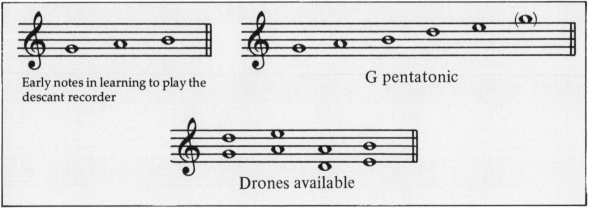

Early notes in learning to play the descant recorder

G pentatonic

Drones available

How to identify a particular 'major' pentatonic on an instrument:
Find the group of three notes with consecutive letter names. Here it is G, A, B. The left-hand note of the three gives the scale its name. The comparable 'minor' pentatonic is the next lower note in the scale. Here it is E

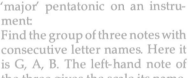

G pentatonic

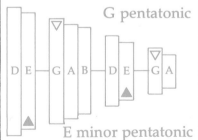

E minor pentatonic

HOW TO INTEGRATE TUNED PERCUSSION AND RECORDERS

◆ Substitute chime bars or other tuned percussion if necessary

◆◆ Repeat the phrase on A's, then on G's.

◆◆◆ Follow by echoes (singing and recorders).

FINAL SHAPE OF THE PIECE

Section A : Rondo Theme   f
    (Suo-gân)

Section B : First Episode
    (Recorder echo c
    work)

Section A : Rondo Theme   f

Section C : Second Episode
    (Phrase/Response
    patterns on
    recorders) e

Section A : Rondo Theme   f

Add drone and accompaniments (the same as for the B section if you wish)

Suo Gân

HOW TO IMPROVISE A PENTATONIC RONDO BASED ON AN EXISTING SONG

4. Many song books contain a pentatonic song or two, and there are several pentatonic song books on the market (see the list on page 43). A pentatonic song offers a good framework for improvisation in that children can add drones and ostinato pattern accompaniments of their own, and make up interludes, all based on the same scale as that of the song. Be warned, though, that some pentatonic songs, though they keep to the notes of a particular pentatonic scale, are really based on chords, and are more suited to guitar accompaniment, for example. For instance, in Brian Brocklehurst's *Pentatonic Song Book* (Schott), No. 16, ("The Mocking Bird") is really based on two chords in G major, even though all its notes are in G pentatonic. Avoid these for pentatonic improvisations.

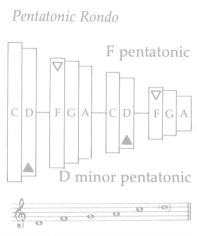

Canoe Round
Melody by Margaret Embers McGee (1918)

◆ Indicate voice entries if sung as a ROUND

Verse 2:
Dip-dip and swing her back,
Flashing with silver,
Follow the wild goose track,
Dip-dip and swing.

◆◆These echoes illustrate a considerable advance on the basic work shown earlier in the book

FINAL SHAPE OF THE PIECE

A   Rondo Texture (Existing tune plus accompaniments)

B   First Episode (Echo patterns on tuned instruments)

A   Rondo Texture

C   Drum Solo improvisation

A   Rondo Texture (Tune sung as a round at a bar's distance)

ORGANISATION OF A PENTATONIC RONDO

5(a) Teach the chosen pentatonic song, ensuring that the words are sung clearly.

(b) Add an appropriate drone on a low-pitched tuned percussion instrument.

(c) Add an appropriate ostinato accompaniment on a high- or middle-pitched tuned instrument. If this is new work for the children, let them suggest a pattern of words from the song upon which to base its rhythm. Take into account the nature of the instrument. (See page 21, 8e)

(d) Choose techniques for the EPISODES: (see diagram right).

(e) Some pentatonic tunes work well as ROUNDS (See *Catch a Round* in this series). If this is the case, it is often effective to treat the tune in this way for the last appearance of the rondo texture.

Phrase/Response
or Echo Patterns
or Improvisation

ON

Tuned Instruments
or Untuned Instruments
or Recorders
or Voices

ACCOMPANIED BY

The same drone used in the RONDO, (A section)
or a new drone on a tuned percussion instrument.

AND/OR

the tuned ostinato used in the RONDO
or another
or an untuned ostinato

Suggestions for techniques for episodes.

Two tips on Organisation

1. Don't feel guilty because only a limited number of children are able to play on a xylophone in any one music lesson. To identify those children who are able to manage a particular rhythm, get the whole class to play it on their knees (knee-slapping). This is quicker than, and preferable to asking just the required number for a particular task, and then finding out that one of them can't manage it. The children don't know that you are going to ask them to transfer the rhythm to a percussion instrument (tuned or untuned). Everyone should, of course, have his turn at playing something at some time, at his own level. If at all possible, tuned percussion instruments should be available for children's practice during break-time or at any other suitable time.

2. When beginning group music-making in class, it is worth working with a small group of children (to help them practise their parts) at any time you can manage other than during the music lesson. This well-practised exercise can then become part of an improvisation in the lesson at a considerable saving of time, compared with trying to teach the parts with all the other children present.

Music for Listening

Children learn the shape of a musical form when they improvise a piece using that form. When they have worked out a Ternary Form piece (ABA) or a Rondo (ABACA is one of several possibilities) encourage them to listen to recorded music using the same form. The following are just a few examples

Ternary form

Debussy: *En Bateau*
Mozart: Serenade in G (No. 13) for Strings, K. 525, ("Eine kleine Nachtmusik"), Third Movement Symphony 39 in E flat (K. 543), Third Movement
Prokofiev: Classical Symphony, Second and Third Movements
Schubert: Symphony 5 in B flat, Third Movement
Schumann: Träumerei

Rondo

Beethoven: *Sonata in G, Op. 79, Vivace*
Couperin: *"The Harvesters" (Sixth Harpsichord Suite)*
Haydn: *Gipsy Rondo*
Kodaly: *"Viennese Musical Clock" (Second Movement of "Hary Janos" Suite.)*
Mozart: *Sonata 11 in A, K. 331— "Rondo Alla Turca"
Rondo in D, K. 485, for Piano
Piano Concerto in c minor, K. 457, Finale*
Rameau: *Musette en Rondeau (1724)*

Recommended Related Material

The Last Month of the Year: John Odom, Schott (Numbers 2, 3 and 7 are particularly useful in the Junior School.)

Books containing Pentatonic Tunes:

Pentatonic Song Book. *(Brocklehurst), Schott 10909a*
The Second Pentatonic Song Book. *(Brocklehurst), Schott 11344a*
Songs for Schools. *(Bissell), Schott 4164*
Music for Children, Vol. 1. *(Orff/Murray), Schott 4865*
Just Five!, Books 1 and 2. *(Kersey), Belwin-Mills*

NOTE: Many of these songs are rather long for use in the ways suggested in this book. Try accompanying rounds where the second voice part enters a short distance after the first (about one bar) with pentatonic accompaniments: many will work well.